SAILING TO AMERICA

Colonists at Sea

by James E. Knight

illustrated by George Guzzi

Sailing to America is the fictional account of the ship Treadwell's *voyage across the Atlantic. It is drawn from the journals and reports of actual journeys, which took place during the 1600s.*

Cover art by Shi Chen.

Library of Congress Cataloging-in-Publication Data

Knight, James E.
    Sailing to America.
    Summary: Describes the 1633 voyage of the ship
Treadwell carrying Puritans and other colonists from
England to the New World.
    1. America—Discovery and exploration—English—
Juvenile literature.   2. Ocean travel—Juvenile literature.
[1. United States—History—Colonial period, ca. 1600-1775.
2. United States—Emigration and Immigration.
3. Ocean travel—History. 4. Puritans.]
I. Guzzi, George, ill.   II. Title.
E127.K58   973.2   81-23161
ISBN 0-89375-726-8   AACR2
ISBN 0-8167-4555-2 (pbk.)

This edition published 1998 by Troll Communications L.L.C.

Printed in the United States of America.

10   9   8   7   6   5

ADVENTURES IN COLONIAL AMERICA

SAILING TO AMERICA

Colonists at Sea

"Tim-m-ber!" shouted the Chief Forester. With a thunderous roar that seemed to shake the Hampshire forest for miles around, the mighty oak tree crashed to the ground. "Prune it, and haul it away," ordered the Chief Forester.

Woodsmen sprang forward and began chopping off the huge tree's branches. Soon the thick straight trunk was ready to be taken to the shipyard near the English seaport of Southampton. Hampshire oak was the finest in the land. It made the best planking for the hulls of English merchant ships.

A team of oxen dragged the great log to the shipyard. Here, on the southern coast of England, the Pilgrim ship *Mayflower* had been built some forty years before.

The log was rolled over a pit called a "saw pit." Then two men began sawing it into planks. One man stood on top of the log, and the other stood below—in the pit. Hour after hour, they pulled a long steel bucksaw up and down. With each motion, sawdust fell into the deep pit. By the end of the following day, there was a huge pile of sawdust and eight rough planks.

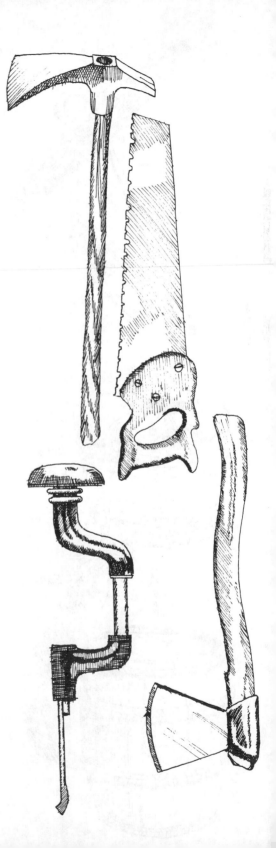

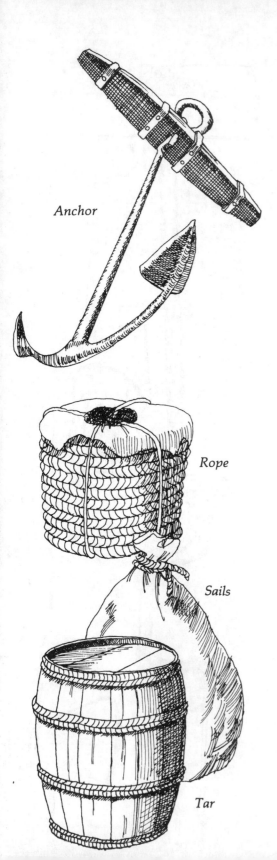

Anchor

Rope

Sails

Tar

The skeleton of a new ship stood nearby in the shipyard. Its keel, or backbone, had been laid, and its bare ribs were already fastened in place—ready for planking. The eight new planks were smoothed and shaped. Next, they were softened with steam, so they could be bent to the shape of the ship's hull. Then shipwrights fastened the oak planks to the ribs. The wood was still green, but it was often used that way—especially when a new ship was needed in a hurry.

This new ship *was* needed in a hurry. It already had a name—the *Treadwell*, after its future owner, Sir Richard Treadwell. Sir Richard was a shipping merchant, who needed a new cargo ship as soon as possible.

Before long, the *Treadwell* was fully planked. The ship's seams were caulked, or sealed, with hot tar. The decks were laid, and the boat was painted. Then the *Treadwell* was launched and fitted with three oak masts and yardarms to support the sails. Next the workers built the bowsprit, the long wooden beam extending over the water from the front of the ship. Smiths installed special metal fittings, and the anchors were hauled aboard.

6

Carpenters completed their work on the holds and compartments below decks. Miles of sturdy hemp lines were brought from the ropeworks. The sailmakers finished sewing the heavy canvas sails. And soon, the *Treadwell* was ready for sea.

Like the *Mayflower*, which it resembled in many ways, the *Treadwell* was a square-rigged ship, so named because

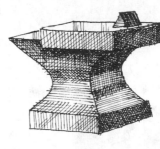

of its large square sails. The *Treadwell* was used to carry goods between Europe and England. But after a year or so, Sir Richard became displeased with the ship. With its blunt bow and stubby hull, the square-rigger was not fast enough to suit him. He decided to use smaller, faster vessels in his business. But what was he to do with the *Treadwell?* The answer came soon enough. The *Treadwell* would carry passengers to America, where they would settle.

So the *Treadwell* was tied to a pier in Southampton, to be fitted out for the long voyage across the Atlantic. It took three weeks for food, water, and other supplies to be packed in large barrels and brought aboard. They were stowed away in the foul-smelling holds below.

It had taken many months for the leaders of this expedition to gather together the people who had decided to settle in Massachusetts—the *Treadwell's* destination. But now there were one hundred passengers ready to leave —about the same number that had sailed on the *Mayflower* just thirteen years before. And sixty-seven of these people were Puritans—members of a religious group.

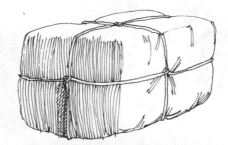

The Puritans believed that the Church of England no longer taught the right way to worship. Because of their strict ways and their criticism of the King, Puritans were not allowed to live in peace. Some had had their land and possessions taken away, and many had been sent to jail. Their lives had become so difficult that they decided to go to the New World to live in the Puritan community that John Winthrop had started. In America they could work hard and live a simple life. They could worship as they pleased, and raise their children in their own faith.

In 1629, King Charles I had granted the Puritans a legal charter to settle in the New World. There they would be able to govern themselves in the name of England. The King was eager to start as many English settlements as possible—and besides, this was a perfect way to get rid of these bothersome Puritans!

So the Puritans' leader, John Winthrop, became governor of the Massachusetts Bay Colony. He had sailed for America with a large group of followers in 1630. Now, more and more English people were making the dangerous trip across the stormy Atlantic to join him.

John Winthrop

Some called the new colonists "Separatists," because they had separated completely from the Church of England. They were even more rigid in their beliefs than Winthrop's group. Many of the passengers who planned to sail aboard the *Treadwell* were Separatists.

So, early one morning in 1633, the *Treadwell*'s passengers came aboard and crowded into their cramped quarters below decks. The ceilings were so low that even women and children found that they had to stoop to walk.

There was very little unused space on the ship. Barrels of provisions, equipment, and the passengers' belongings were stored everywhere.

The voyagers knew the trip would not be an easy one. There would be few comforts and little privacy. Each passenger had bunk space barely large enough for one person to lie down upon. And whenever they tried to move, the travelers found themselves bumping into each other. Below the poorly lit, stuffy living quarters, the passengers could hear the scratching of rats and the sloshing of bilge water. From the decks above, they could hear the sailors moving briskly about, readying the ship for the long trip.

What would the colonists find in the New World? They did not know. But many of the *Treadwell's* passengers hoped to find land to farm in America. There were some who wanted to work at trades, such as carpentry, leathermaking, or masonry. A few were going because they could not pay their debts. They believed an uncertain future in America was better than going to debtor's prison in England.

14

Somehow, most of the passengers had been able to scrape together enough money to pay for their trip to the New World. But a few could not pay. Still, they were determined to start their lives anew in America. So they had signed indentures, or contracts, in which they agreed to become servants for several years to pay for their trip. They were called *indentured servants*.

The morning breeze filled the *Treadwell*'s sails, and the ship sailed out of Southampton. The passengers crowded to the rails for a last look at England. Back at the docks, relatives and friends were waving to them. It was a sad, yet joyous good-bye. Many of the future colonists realized they would probably never again see those they left behind. And yet, they welcomed the challenge of beginning a new life in America.

Once at sea, the *Treadwell* began to pitch and roll in the rough waves of the North Atlantic Ocean. The ship creaked and groaned. The sails strained before the wind. When the weather was bad, the passengers were not allowed to go on deck. It was too dangerous. But even in their cramped quarters below, they were tossed about. There was barely room enough to breathe. They could not walk, sit, or even lie down on their bunks comfortably. Many became seasick.

The passengers had brought a great many belongings

with them, which made the overcrowded conditions worse. Most voyagers had large, wooden chests bound with strips of brass. In them, they had crammed clothing and other articles they would need in the New World. Some mothers had taken along their babies' cradles. As the ship rolled, the passengers could not help tripping and stumbling over the chests and cradles.

Many farmers had brought along their favorite scythes and spades wrapped in cloth. To save space, the wooden handles had been removed and left behind. They would be replaced when the ship reached America. Women had brought along their iron pots and other utensils to cook with in their new homeland. Carpenters had brought their precious tools. Everyone had heard how scarce iron, steel, and other metals were in the New World.

The future colonists had also brought along livestock —pigs, cows, oxen, and chickens. They were kept in one of the lower holds of the *Treadwell*. Most of these animals would not survive the long trip to Massachusetts. The air in the hold was so bad that many would grow sick and die. Others would have to be killed for food.

During its first month at sea, the *Treadwell* ran into bad weather and high seas. But these were nothing compared to the fierce storm that struck the ship during the fifth week. Gale winds and heavy rains hit the *Treadwell* with such force that those aboard thought the ship would surely sink. The wild Atlantic seemed to be set on destroying the little square-rigger.

Monstrous waves rose like mountains around the *Treadwell*. Tons of sea water pounded across the decks. The wind howled through the rigging. A hatch cover was ripped off and blown over the side. Icy water poured down into the passengers' quarters.

The captain was afraid the strong winds would rip the sails to shreds. He sent his crew up into the rigging, to roll up the sails against the yardarms. Slowly, the sailors crept up high above the rocking deck and began taking in the canvas.

The men had just finished their work when someone shouted, "Man overboard!" A huge wave had swept one young sailor into the angry sea. A line was heaved over the side. Somehow the sailor managed to grab it and hold on. Crew members frantically pulled on the line, dragging their shipmate closer and closer to the side of the *Treadwell*. Finally, they hauled him back on board the ship.

The storm continued to rage. For the next few days, the *Treadwell* was tossed helplessly about. With the gale still blowing, the captain did not dare to unfurl the sails. So the ship was swept far off course.

Below, in their closely-packed quarters, the new colonists rode out the storm as best they could. Frightened mothers tried to comfort crying babies. Nearly everyone was seasick. As the little ship rolled in the wild seas, people were thrown out of their bunks, tumbling over each other. Moans and cries filled the foul air. Some people prayed silently. Many prayed aloud. Others cursed the day they had ever decided to go on such a terrible ocean voyage.

Finally, the storm ended, and the weather cleared. The captain ordered the sails set once again. Sailors scrambled up into the rigging.

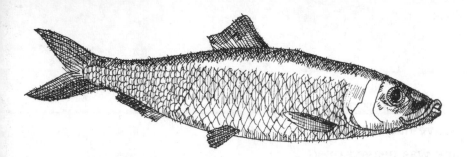

Dried Beef

Cheese

Biscuits

Some of the passengers gave thanks, and tried to make some order of the confusion below deck. Others crowded on deck to fill their lungs with fresh air. At last, the children were free to run and play in the open air.

The voyagers ate the same food day after day. Their diet consisted of dried beef, smoked fish, cheese, and "hardtack"—dried biscuit. The pieces of meat were old, dirty, and so heavily salted that the passengers had to force them down their throats.

The cheese was also old—and green with mold. There was no way to keep it cool and fresh. So people just scraped the mold off, and tried to make the best of a difficult situation.

Soon the ship's supply of biscuits had spoiled. "In a single biscuit," wrote one passenger in his diary, "it is hard to find a piece the size of a penny that does not have worms in it." Sometimes there was ale to wash the biscuits down—but it was always stale. The drinking water served to the passengers was muddy-looking, smelly, and often filled with worms.

As the *Treadwell* entered its third month at sea, the

22

supply of food and water grew dangerously low. The captain ordered the daily rations to be cut. The mighty ocean still lay all about them, and no one could say how much longer the trip would take.

Only the passengers' great hunger and thirst forced
them to eat and drink the food and water that was put
before them. And as they did so each day, they risked
their very lives. For the food and water were so bad that
they carried germs that made even the strongest
passengers sick. Bathing or washing clothes was
impossible—the water supply was too low.

As the *Treadwell* began its tenth week at sea, illness and disease spread through the ship. People began to bleed at the gums, and then they grew weak and ill. These were the signs of scurvy. At that time, no one knew what caused this disease. More than a century later, the cause of scurvy would be discovered to be a lack of fresh fruits and vegetables. Aboard the *Treadwell*, many who did not get scurvy suffered from other illnesses—fever, boils, and colds. Seasickness continued to torment nearly everyone. And so did lice and rats.

Only one person aboard the *Mayflower* had died on the voyage to the New World. The *Treadwell* was not so lucky—eleven people were lost. Children were the first to die. Many youngsters caught measles and smallpox. They tossed and sweated in their bunks for a few days—and then were gone. The ship's doctor could do little for them.

Some of the passengers could not force themselves to swallow the bad food or to drink the evil-looking water—so they died of hunger or thirst. As on the *Mayflower*, a woman gave birth aboard the *Treadwell*.

But the infant could not survive amid the sickness and disease. In good weather, the religious leaders read services over the bodies of those who had died, and they were buried at sea.

In spite of the hardships, most of the colonists survived. But there was one enemy no one could escape—boredom. Week after endless week at sea with nothing to do made people short-tempered. Wives and husbands quarreled. So did brothers and sisters. Sailors picked fights with each other—and sometimes with the passengers. Many aboard the ship were homesick. They longed for the comforts they had left behind in England.

Yet, despite the suffering aboard the *Treadwell*, there were some good times, too. On sunny days when the seas were quiet, the passengers and crew would gather on the deck to gossip and to wonder out loud about what life would be like in Massachusetts. Children played games and watched the sailors carve small designs on pieces of wood. Cooking was allowed on such days, and the passengers heated their rations of salted beef over wood coals.

The leaders among the passengers were wise. They knew that everyone aboard the ship had gone through terrible hardships. So to keep the people's spirits up, they held "hymn-sings" on deck. They preached sermons and held frequent prayer meetings. Passages from the Bible were read out loud. The sick were carried up from their stuffy quarters below, and as they listened to the sermons, they breathed the fresh sea air. Sometimes the young sailors made everyone laugh by doing a lively dance to a tune played upon a *hornpipe*, a small instrument made of wood and horn.

As the days passed, the colonists' hopes began to rise. Surely, they told each other, the long voyage must soon come to an end. Many would stare out over the water day after day. They were watching for birds, for they knew that where there were birds, there was sure to be land nearby.

On the *Treadwell*'s ninety-first day at sea, nearly everyone was on deck. It was a fine, sunny afternoon, and a fair breeze was carrying the ship along at a good speed. Every sail was set and pulling well.

Something strange and mysterious was in the air. Everyone seemed to sense it. People sniffed. It was as if the smell of earth was in the wind.

Might this be the day? they asked themselves.

Suddenly, a lookout in the main crow's nest shouted, "Land! Land ho!"

The mate on deck jumped to his feet. "Where away?" he called.

"Two points off the larboard bow, sir," yelled the lookout. "I see it clearly."

Soon everyone could see it—low green hills, trees, and a white sandy beach. They had finally reached the coast of Massachusetts! The captain checked his charts. Their destination was the Bay Colony port of Plymouth. He could not tell exactly how close they now were to the colony. They would have to wait until tomorrow morning—then they would search for it.

No one seemed to mind the delay. After nearly three months, they had finally seen land! People laughed and hugged each other. Some fell to their knees and offered thanks that the long and difficult voyage was nearly over. Many wept for joy. The sick were carried up on deck to see the shores of their new homeland.

In a high, thin voice, someone began to sing a Puritan hymn. One by one, everybody—captain, crew, and passengers—joined in.

The *Treadwell* had brought its cargo of new colonists safely across the wide Atlantic to the New World.

They had made it to America!

Index